WHAT'S DRIVING YOUR LIFE?

A 10-Day Turnaround for a Fresh Start

RICK WARREN

A Tyndale nonfiction imprint

Visit Tyndale online at tyndale.com.

Visit Tyndale Momentum online at tyndalemomentum.com.

Visit Rick Warren online at PastorRick.com.

Tyndale, Tyndale's quill logo, *Tyndale Momentum*, and the Tyndale Momentum logo are registered trademarks of Tyndale House Ministries. Tyndale Momentum is a nonfiction imprint of Tyndale House Publishers, Carol Stream, Illinois.

What's Driving Your Life?: A 10-Day Turnaround for a Fresh Start

Copyright © 2024 by Rick Warren. All rights reserved.

Devotions are taken from the *Daily Hope Devotional*, published by Tyndale House Publishers in 2024 under ISBN 979-8-4005-0112-8.

Cover photograph of abstract painting by Henrik Dønnestad on Unsplash.

Cover and interior illustration of sunrise logo copyright © Leone_V/Shutterstock. All rights reserved.

Designed by Dean H. Renninger

For information about special discounts for bulk purchases, please contact Tyndale House Publishers at csresponse@tyndale.com, or call 1-855-277-9400.

ISBN 979-8-4005-0458-7

Printed by **novus print**, a division of Novus Holdings

30 29 28 27 26 25 24
7 6 5 4 3 2 1

Contents

Introduction 1

....

DAY 1: *A Fresh Start That Turns Anxiety to Peace 9*

DAY 2: *A Fresh Start Focused on God's Provision 13*

DAY 3: *A Fresh Start Rooted in Transformed Thoughts 17*

DAY 4: *A Fresh Start to Extend Grace in Relationships 21*

DAY 5: *A Fresh Start for Pursuing Your Identity 25*

DAY 6: *A Fresh Start to Face the Future without Fear 29*

DAY 7: *A Fresh Start for When You Fail 33*

DAY 8: *A Fresh Start Built on Renewal, Not Stress 37*

DAY 9: *A Fresh Start That Relies on Divine Direction 41*

DAY 10: *A Fresh Start That Leads to Rest 45*

....

Next Steps 49
God's Promises to You 57
Scripture Credits 73
About the Author 75

Introduction

The world is moving at a frantic pace, and you may feel the pressure of staying one step ahead—or maybe just keeping up. Perhaps you are trying to make sense of your life and add a little meaning to each day. While it may feel like you're being pulled along by your circumstances, you are actually the one who decides what you allow to drive your life—**and everyone is driven by something.**

The word *drive* means to guide, control, or direct. For instance, if you drive a nail into wood with a hammer, you guide, control, and direct the nail into the wood. If you drive a car, you guide, control, and direct the car down the street.

What's driving you?

Right now, you may be driven by a problem, a pressure, or a deadline. Or perhaps you're driven by guilt, resentment, fear, materialism, or the need for approval. There are hundreds of circumstances, values, and emotions that can drive your life, and every one of them makes you weary.

Maybe you're driven by current events, and you're looking for meaning in things that will not last. You feel the tension of a polarized society and rapidly advancing technology, and you've taken on an emotional load that you were never meant to carry.

Even religion can drive your life, leaving you worn out and aimless. Why? Because religion is humanity's attempt to get to God. It's a list of rules, regulations, and restrictions that people think they should follow to make God smile.

INTRODUCTION

But Jesus is God's plan to get to humanity. Jesus didn't say, "I've come to give you religion." He said, *"I have come that they may have life, and have it to the full"* (John 10:10, NIV).

There are hundreds of forces that can drive your life, but all lead to the same end: unused potential, unnecessary stress, and an unfulfilled life.

You need a purpose greater than yourself to drive your life.

Nothing can compensate for traveling through life without knowing your purpose—not success, wealth, fame, or pleasure. Without purpose, your life will always feel like motion without meaning, activity without direction.

When you have no clear purpose, you have no road map to help guide your decisions, allocate your time, and manage your resources. You'll keep changing directions, jobs, relationships, or churches, hoping each change will settle the confusion or fill the emptiness in your heart.

WHAT'S DRIVING YOUR LIFE?

The only way you'll ever get a clear purpose for your life is to talk to God, the one who made you, and read the Bible, the owner's manual for life. You didn't create yourself, so there is no way you can determine what you were created to do!

The Bible says, *"Everything, absolutely everything . . . got started in him and finds its purpose in him"* (Colossians 1:16, MSG).

God wants your life to be driven by *his* purposes—the five things he put you on earth to do:

- know and love him
- belong to his family
- grow in faith
- serve others
- tell others about him

That's what life is all about!

The truth is, you can't do everything people

want you to do and everything this world says you *should* be able to do. You have just the right amount of time to do God's will and pursue the purposes he created you for. You don't have the energy to give your devotion and your focus to many different things, even if those things are good.

The Bible says, *"Give yourselves completely to God, for you were dead, but now you have new life. So use your whole body as an instrument to do what is right for the glory of God"* (Romans 6:13, NLT).

Giving your life to Jesus and following God with your whole heart isn't about doing more or being dragged down by rules and restrictions. It's about understanding that you were made for a relationship with him. And when you know God and trust him with your future, he gives you his wisdom and a new perspective on your pain. He helps you turn from pursuing things that will never satisfy you to focusing instead on *his* way. He reveals his purpose, one step at a time.

He gives you a fresh start.

If you're feeling exhausted, frustrated, and unsettled today, I have good news! God has not left you alone to figure out which way you should go. He has given you his Word to fill your life with purpose and peace and to help you stay on the right path. The Bible says, *"Give us this day our daily bread"* (Matthew 6:11, ESV). That's what God does—he gives *daily* direction.

It's hard to imagine what God might do with your life when you are totally committed to his purposes. Ephesians 3:20 says, *"God can do anything, you know—far more than you could ever imagine or guess or request in your wildest dreams!"* (MSG). His Word will bring you such amazing rest, refreshment, and clarity. And as you draw closer to him, he'll revitalize your soul.

INTRODUCTION

The renewal starts now.

Using this booklet, you'll spend the next ten days discovering what needs to be refreshed in your life and what could use a turnaround. As you pause each day to consider what's driving your life, you'll find out how to get the power to shift your focus from earthly things to eternal things.

Before you begin this ten-day journey, be sure your heart and mind are ready to hear from God. Is there anything that's keeping you from hearing him clearly? We live in a media-saturated world. Have you let doomscrolling or the twenty-four-hour news cycle take up too much of your time or attention? If so, it's time to hit pause on that consumption and make a bold commitment.

Here's the challenge: For the next ten days, switch gears. Instead of being steeped in negativity and distraction, how about dedicating your time to seeking God? Commit to putting aside whatever drowns out God's voice in your life so you can be ready to hear from him. It's time for a fresh start only God can give.

Are you up for the challenge? Take the leap and begin this journey of transformation. As you start hearing God clearly and letting him drive your life, you'll be amazed at the difference it makes in just ten days.

DAY 1

A Fresh Start That Turns Anxiety to Peace

I am leaving you with a gift—peace of mind and heart! And the peace I give isn't fragile like the peace the world gives. So don't be troubled or afraid.

JOHN 14:27 (TLB)

When you make room for Jesus, he gives you one of the greatest gifts: *"I am leaving you with a gift—peace of mind and heart! And the peace I give isn't fragile like the peace the world gives. So don't be troubled or afraid"* (John 14:27, TLB).

The kind of peace the world gives is temporary. In the last three hundred years, hundreds of peace treaties have been signed—and almost none of them have been kept.

The peace that comes from the world is totally circumstantial. If you have a good job, then you're at peace. But if you lose your job, then you're not at peace anymore. If you've got money in the bank, then you're at peace. But when that money is gone, you're not at peace anymore.

Jesus gives you a different kind of peace. The Bible calls it peace that *"surpasses all understanding"* (Philippians 4:7, ESV).

What does that mean? It means you have

DAY 1

peace when there's no obvious or visible reason why you should be at peace. Everything around you could be in chaos, but for some unexplainable reason, you are at peace. That is the peace that surpasses understanding—and it can only come from Jesus, the Prince of Peace.

Jesus wants to give you that kind of peace so you won't be troubled or afraid.

Whenever Jesus walks into a room, he fills that room with peace. Do you have rooms in your heart that are full of worry, disorder, anxiety, or fear? Those are the rooms you haven't invited Jesus into. Your worries reveal the areas you have not surrendered to God. That could include your finances, your dating life, your career, your parenting, your schedule, or your ministry. Whatever it is, you have to let it go. You have to give it over to Jesus.

Here's the only way you're going to have real peace: Give every part of your life to God to use for his purposes. Then you'll have peace that will stand up to all of life's pressures.

....

Pray: *God, I want to have the kind of peace that surpasses understanding and replaces my fear with confidence and my worry with rest. I know there are rooms in my heart that need to be evaluated with humility and honesty. There are parts of my life that have only brought disorder and chaos, and I want them to be under your control. Please reveal to me the areas that I have not submitted to you so that I can surrender them fully and experience lasting peace.*

DAY 2

....

A Fresh Start Focused on God's Provision

....

Remember the LORD your God,
for it is he who gives you the ability
to produce wealth, and so confirms his covenant,
which he swore to your ancestors, as it is today.

DEUTERONOMY 8:18 (NIV)

WHAT'S DRIVING YOUR LIFE?

The Bible teaches that God is the source of our finances. He is the one who provides for our needs.

Deuteronomy 8:18 says, *"Remember the LORD your God, for it is he who gives you the ability to produce wealth, and so confirms his covenant, which he swore to your ancestors, as it is today"* (NIV).

So what does that mean for your everyday life?

It means that instead of looking to your employer for financial security, you look to God. It means that instead of looking to your savings account for financial security, you look to God. Instead of looking to your investments or assets, you look to God. It means that you don't depend on anyone or anything other than God to provide for your needs.

Let me illustrate it this way: When you turn on the water at your kitchen sink, you know the water doesn't actually come from the faucet.

DAY 2

The water comes *through* the faucet. The water comes from a reservoir or a well, and the way you happen to receive it is through the faucet.

In the same way, the income that God wants to give you may come through a job or an investment or through something or someone else.

But the source is always God.

You don't need to worry about which faucet God uses to supply your needs. In a sense he says, "If I turn off one faucet, I can just as easily turn on another. If you lose one job, I can give you another. Your job isn't your source. Your bank account isn't your source. I am your source."

Maybe you feel like your faucet has run dry. But because you know God's supply will never run dry, you can trust that he has already chosen another way to provide for you.

Worry reveals the places where we aren't trusting God. Ask him to help you identify those areas where you struggle to trust him. Pray for more faith to trust that he will supply everything you need to do his will.

Then, look for the "faucets" he uses to meet your needs.

....

Pray: *Lord, I want to trust you to provide for all my needs because I know everything I have is from you. Right now, I'm wondering how I'm going to make it through my current financial challenges. But you have always made a way for me in the past, and you have promised in your Word that you will give me all I need to fulfill my purpose. So I will look to you and expect you to provide for me again. Please give me patience as I wait on you and your perfect timing.*

DAY 3

A Fresh Start Rooted in Transformed Thoughts

Happy are those who . . . find joy in obeying the Law of the LORD, and they study it day and night. They are like trees that grow beside a stream, that bear fruit at the right time, and whose leaves do not dry up. They succeed in everything they do.

PSALM 1:1-3 (GNT)

WHAT'S DRIVING YOUR LIFE?

If you want to change your life, then start by changing the way you think.

Changing your thoughts is the key to a fresh start in any area—a hobby, career, relationship, marriage, or parenting. Ephesians 4:23 says, *"Be renewed in the spirit of your minds"* (ESV).

Having a renewed mind means you have fresh thoughts and fresh attitudes. It means you take your wrong attitudes and thoughts and surrender them, letting *"God transform you inwardly by a complete change of your mind"* (Romans 12:2, GNT).

You renew your mind by doing two things:

First, listen to God's Word more than the world. The Bible says, *"Happy are those who . . . find joy in obeying the Law of the LORD, and they study it day and night. They are like trees that grow beside a stream, that bear fruit at the right time, and whose leaves do not dry up. They succeed in everything they do"* (Psalm 1:1-3, GNT).

DAY 3

Would you like those characteristics to be true in your life? If so, then meditate on God's Word every day.

Second, think about what you think about. Instead of automatically accepting every thought you have, challenge your thoughts. When you have a thought, ask yourself: "Do I *want* to think about this? Is this true? Is this helpful? How does it make me feel—and do I want to feel that way?"

The Bible tells us to *"take every thought captive and make it obey Christ"* (2 Corinthians 10:5, GNT). All your feelings start with a thought. What you think about is your choice, and you don't have to believe every thought you have. When you confront a thought you know isn't true, you can replace it with God's truth. The only way to know the truth is to read God's Word.

WHAT'S DRIVING YOUR LIFE?

Start changing your thoughts today. It will give you a fresh start, and it will change your life!

....

Pray: *Father, when my thoughts and attitudes aren't rooted in your Word, I can easily become discouraged, self-focused, or impatient. I want to know you and your Word better, so today I ask for the Holy Spirit's help to be more disciplined in my Bible study and quiet time and to meditate on your Word throughout the day. Please fill my mind with your love and truth so that I can live out my purpose and find joy in loving you and others well.*

DAY 4

....

A Fresh Start to Extend Grace in Relationships

....

Always be humble and gentle. Be patient with each other, making allowance for each other's faults because of your love.

EPHESIANS 4:2 (NLT)

WHAT'S DRIVING YOUR LIFE?

No relationship will survive without grace. You've got to cut people some slack! You've got to let things go.

The Bible says, *"Love patiently accepts all things"* (1 Corinthians 13:7, NCV). In the original Greek, the basic meaning of the word translated *"patiently accepts"* is to "cover with a roof." Would you buy a house without a roof? Of course not. You'd have no protection from wind and rain. A roof covers and protects your home.

In the same way, biblical love covers a relationship and lets some things slide. It doesn't hold people accountable for every little mistake they make. You need a roof on your relationship because people are damaged pretty easily, and we need the kind of love that extends grace.

Why is grace essential to relationships?

Because we are all sinners. If you're married, you married a sinner—and your spouse

DAY 4

did too! Two imperfect spouses will never make a perfect marriage. And it's the same way in friendships. No friendship is perfect—because no friend is perfect. Two imperfect people will never create a perfect relationship.

The Bible says in Romans 3:10, *"There is no one who always does what is right, not even one"* (NCV). Nobody gets it right 100 percent of the time. It's rarely just one person's fault. We all make mistakes, and there's always responsibility on both sides. The saying goes, "It takes two to tango." It also takes two to disagree!

That's why the Bible says we have to learn to extend grace to each other. Forgiveness is a two-way street. We cannot receive what we're unwilling to give to other people.

You build strong relationships by treating other people the way God treats you. Romans 15:7 says, *"Accept each other just as Christ has accepted you"* (NLT). Accepting others may include listening to a friend without judging, or giving space to a tired, grumpy family member.

When you accept others as they are, looking past their faults for the sake of love, that's extending grace.

....

Pray: *Lord, each day you offer me unlimited love, forgiveness, and grace. As I try to become more like you and strengthen my relationships, I want to accept people the way you've accepted me. But I don't always find it easy to be so generous to others—especially those who've hurt me. Please remind me that I don't have to have the last word, and I don't have to point out every mistake. Help me to let little things go and to seek wise counsel for any deeper hurts that are keeping me stuck.*

DAY 5

....

A Fresh Start for Pursuing Your Identity

....

Our purpose is to please God, not people.
He alone examines the motives of our hearts.

1 THESSALONIANS 2:4 (NLT)

WHAT'S DRIVING YOUR LIFE?

God made you to be *you*. He didn't make you to be what your parents, spouse, boss, or friends want you to be.

God wants you to be exactly who he created you to be. That means you have to refuse to be defined by others.

Hebrews 11:24 says, *"By faith Moses, when he had grown up, refused to be known as the son of Pharaoh's daughter"* (NIV). Moses had an identity crisis. He was born a Hebrew slave but raised as Egyptian royalty, the grandson of Pharaoh. When he grew up, he had two choices: He could pretend to be Pharaoh's grandson for the rest of his life and live with luxury, fame, and power.

Or he could admit who he really was: a Hebrew. If he did, his family would kick him out to live with slaves for the rest of his life. He would be disgraced and humiliated and live a life of pain and drudgery.

Which would you choose?

DAY 5

Most people today are living lies—trying to be people they're not. But Moses refused to live a lie because he was a man of integrity. Against all kinds of peer pressure, he insisted on being who God made him to be.

Who are you letting determine your identity?

Some people's parents died years ago, but they're still trying to live up to their expectations. Some people are hanging on to what their ex-husband or ex-wife said, trying to prove that person wrong. Some people are striving to keep up with what the culture says they should be. But the Bible says this: *"Our purpose is to please God, not people. He alone examines the motives of our hearts"* (1 Thessalonians 2:4, NLT).

Choose to be who God made you to be. Simply say, "I resolve to no longer let other people press me into their mold. I'm going to do what God wants me to do and fulfill the plan he has for my life—not somebody else's plan for my life."

That is true success in life. God wants you to be exactly who he created you to be—nothing more.

....

Pray: *God, thank you that I don't have to try to be anything other than who you made me to be. I need your wisdom to pursue the things that help me fulfill my purpose and make me more like you. When I'm tempted to act a certain way because I think it will gain someone's approval, please bring to mind your Word and the truth that my only purpose is to please you, not people. I want my success to be defined by how I faithfully follow and honor you.*

DAY 6

....

A Fresh Start to Face the Future without Fear

....

The LORD watches over all who love him.

PSALM 145:20 (NIV)

When you put your trust in Jesus, you never need to fear the future. His goodness and mercy are with you every day.

You're following the Good Shepherd, and he is out in front of you with his rod and staff. And at the back of the flock are a couple of sheepdogs—goodness and mercy—nudging you along, making sure you don't stray away.

God's goodness is watching over you. Did you know a second hasn't passed in your life when God wasn't watching you? God is always paying attention to you because he created you to love you. He knows every detail of your life. Psalm 145:20 says, *"The LORD watches over all who love him"* (NIV).

Not only does he watch over you, but he also protects you. The Bible says, *"God will command his angels to protect you wherever you go"* (Psalm 91:11, CEV).

DAY 6

God's protection doesn't mean that only good things will happen to you. Disappointment and pain will still come your way. But God promises that good will come out of everything that happens to you—whether or not you're able to see in this lifetime how he has worked.

God's mercy and grace are working in you. The Bible says in Isaiah 60:10, *"I will have mercy on you through my grace"* (TLB).

Grace is when God gives you what you don't deserve. Mercy is when God *doesn't* give you what you *do* deserve. For all the ways you've sinned, failed, and made mistakes, you deserve punishment, yet God pardons and forgives you through Christ. That's mercy.

It is God's nature to be merciful. He loves to show his mercy! He doesn't get tired of it. He doesn't get frustrated when you keep coming back for more.

WHAT'S DRIVING YOUR LIFE?

The truth is, God is with you every moment of every day, always offering his goodness and mercy.

Nobody knows what's going to happen next week, much less in the next decade. But when you face the future, remember this: God will fill your life to overflowing, and his goodness and mercy will be with you. There is no need to fear.

....

Pray: *Father, you are so kind to walk with me through my trials and show me your goodness. I don't have to look behind me in fear, and I can look to the future with confidence, because you know everything and are working everything for good. Thank you for knowing me and never running out of grace and mercy. Please help me to look at my circumstances through the lens of your goodness so I remember that I am not alone.*

DAY 7

....

A Fresh Start for When You Fail

....

Forget the former things; do not dwell on the past. See, I am doing a new thing! Now it springs up; do you not perceive it? I am making a way in the wilderness and streams in the wasteland.

ISAIAH 43:18–19 (NIV)

WHAT'S DRIVING YOUR LIFE?

God is the God of second chances—and hundredth and thousandth chances!

The Bible is full of people who got a second chance. Abraham pretended his wife was his sister because he didn't have faith that God would protect him. Moses murdered someone. Samson gave in to his overpowering feelings of rage and lust. Rahab worked as a prostitute. David committed adultery and then had the woman's husband put to death. And yet every one of these people are in God's "Hall of Faith" in Hebrews 11.

God loves to give second chances. If you had to be perfect to receive God's grace, no one would stand a chance!

One of Job's friends offered this advice on recovering from losses in life and returning to God's original plan: *"Put your heart right, Job. Reach out to God. Put away evil and wrong from your home. Then face the world again, firm and courageous. Then all your troubles will fade*

DAY 7

from your memory, like floods that are past and remembered no more. Your life will be brighter than sunshine at noon, and life's darkest hours will shine like the dawn. You will live secure and full of hope; God will protect you and give you rest" (Job 11:13-18, GNT).

What an amazing promise! When you repent, God always offers another chance—and it's filled with courage, hope, protection, and rest.

If you want to move forward into God's awesome dream for your life, then you're going to have to shut the door on the past. You're going to have to give up your grief, your guilt, and your grudges so that you can move forward in faith.

"Forget the former things; do not dwell on the past. See, I am doing a new thing! Now it springs up; do you not perceive it? I am making a way in the wilderness and streams in the wasteland" (Isaiah 43:18-19, NIV).

Trust God today for your second chance. You'll learn that even the darkest days of your past can shine like the dawn. And in the wasteland of your pain, streams will spring up.

....

Pray: *God, please forgive me for the ways I've fallen short of your plan for me. There are so many things I've held on to that have kept me from pursuing you and your will with my whole heart and mind. Do whatever you need to in my life to put me right with you. Thank you for a fresh start and another chance to become a person of great faith. Help me to let go of my guilt so I can keep moving toward my purpose.*

DAY 8

....

A Fresh Start Built on Renewal, Not Stress

....

Very early in the morning, while it was still dark, Jesus got up, left the house and went off to a solitary place, where he prayed.

MARK 1:35 (NIV)

WHAT'S DRIVING YOUR LIFE?

The key to resisting stress is the very thing some Christians do the least: spending time alone with God. But this spiritual practice is essential to building a resilient spirit and managing chronic stress.

Prayer is a great stress reliever. It's a decompression chamber, where you can release the stress of keeping up appearances and living up to others' expectations. It's how you unload your burdens and admit you can't carry them alone. It's where you're reminded that God is ready and willing to help you with every stressful thing you experience in life.

How do you develop a habit of spending time alone with God? Through practice and repetition. It's not a habit unless you do it over and over again, regularly and consistently.

Jesus developed spiritual habits. The Bible says in Luke 22:39 that it was Jesus' habit to leave Jerusalem and go to the Mount of Olives to pray. And Mark 1:35 says, *"Very early in the morning, while it was still dark, Jesus got up, left the house and went off to a solitary place, where he prayed"* (NIV).

No matter how busy he was, Jesus knew he needed time alone with God to pray. Do you have time like that in your life? Do you ever slow down and get quiet before God so you can reflect and be renewed? If you want to be a resilient person, develop the habit of spending time with God.

While word spread about Jesus and huge crowds of people were coming to hear him speak, Jesus made time alone with God a habit. The Bible says, *"Jesus often slipped away to be alone so he could pray"* (Luke 5:16, NCV). If Jesus felt the need to frequently leave the crowd and get alone with God, then think about how much more we must need that.

Because noise often causes stress, consider starting your morning with God instead of with your phone, TV, or social media. Be still, be quiet, and be open to the work God wants to do in you. Make a habit of meditating on his Word and being in his presence.

....

Pray: *God, I want to be faithful in my spiritual habits, but I need your help! I've let my phone and my responsibilities and my weariness keep me from giving priority to my quiet time with you—even though I know it's the one thing that will improve everything else about my day. Give me wisdom to make choices that move me to spiritual maturity. Please give me the desire, above all else, to spend time with you every day and get to know you and your Word.*

DAY 9

A Fresh Start That Relies on Divine Direction

For anyone out there who doesn't know where you're going, anyone groping in the dark, here's what: Trust in GOD. Lean on your God!

ISAIAH 50:10 (MSG)

WHAT'S DRIVING YOUR LIFE?

On dark days, you need the light of Jesus. When you can't see the way forward, when you're confused or undecided, when you don't know what's best, when you can't figure out what to do next, you need his light.

When you're bewildered, well-meaning people will tell you, "Trust yourself. Just follow your instincts!" But anybody who's tried that knows, at best, you're right only about 50 percent of the time. Your perspective is limited. Your light is weak. It's like using one of those tiny penlights that fit on a key chain—they don't really illuminate anything. And as a result of relying only on yourself, you've probably had difficulty making good decisions.

Instead, here's what the Bible says to do: *"For anyone out there who doesn't know where you're going, anyone groping in the dark, here's what: Trust in GOD. Lean on your God!"* (Isaiah 50:10, MSG). Don't count on your own light. Trust the light of the Lord.

DAY 9

If you want to have God's perspective and viewpoint on your problems, then you need to get to know God through the Bible. You need to read and study and saturate your mind and heart with it, because God's will is always found in his Word.

I'm always amazed at how many people are waiting around for God to give them a sign instead of just reading the directions that he's already given them. If you want to stay on the right path, then you have to study the Bible.

God promises to guide you if you'll let him. He says, *"I'll take the hand of those who don't know the way, who can't see where they're going. I'll be a personal guide to them, directing them through unknown country. I'll be right there to show them what roads to take, make sure they don't fall into the ditch. These are the things I'll be doing for them—sticking with them, not leaving them for a minute"* (Isaiah 42:16, MSG).

WHAT'S DRIVING YOUR LIFE?

Let God be your personal guide, starting right now. You'll never have to stumble around in the dark if you let the light of his Word light up your life.

....

Pray: *Father, as I wonder about—and am tempted to worry about—what is ahead for me, I thank you for your presence, your peace, and your promise to lead and guide me every day of my life. Even though I don't know the future, I know you will give me the next step I need to take, and that is enough for me. I will keep close to you in prayer and in your Word, listening and watching for you and trusting in your good plan.*

DAY 10

....

A Fresh Start That Leads to Rest

....

Come to me and I will give you rest.

MATTHEW 11:28 (CEV)

WHAT'S DRIVING YOUR LIFE?

When Jesus says, *"Come to me and I will give you rest"* (Matthew 11:28, CEV), what kind of rest is he talking about?

Jesus offers a rest for your soul that's much deeper than physical rest—because he knows that the problem you need help with right now is probably not overworked muscles.

When you come to Jesus in your emptiness, what you probably have is an overloaded mind, soul, and spirit. You need rest not just from physical work but from tension, stress, anxiety, hurry, and worry. You need the kind of rest that can't come from taking a good nap or going on vacation.

Most people have a way to unwind when they're physically tired that's different from how they unwind when they're emotionally and spiritually exhausted. Maybe when you're tired, you watch a movie or spend time on your phone. Maybe you have to lie down, or maybe you need to go for a walk. Maybe you choose to spend time with friends, or maybe it's better to be alone.

Those can all be good things—but none of them can restore your soul.

Only God can restore your soul. That's why, when you have soul emptiness, soul depression, or soul overload, Jesus wants you to come to him.

Isaiah 40:29 says, *"He gives power to the tired and worn out, and strength to the weak"* (TLB).

When you're empty inside, culture says you need to do more. You need to make more money, get more things, do more things, travel more places. Go, go, go. More, more, more. But that's probably the very reason you're empty!

Jesus wants you to do the opposite: Don't go. Come to him—and come just as you are.

Your soul will never find rest in anything the world has to offer. That's because your soul was not created to be filled by anything in this world.

WHAT'S DRIVING YOUR LIFE?

You were made for God, and you only find real rest when you bring your weary soul to him.

....

Pray: *Lord, I'm tired! And I know a change in my schedule or finances is not the answer— I need to continually come to you for help and just spend time worshiping you and getting to know you. Help me to reject the world's pressure to prove myself with my work and my busyness and all the solutions it offers for weariness. I want to find true, deep rest in my soul by being filled with your Spirit and turning every worry and weight over to you.*

Next Steps

*A Fresh Start through
Daily Time with God*

....

Are you ready to make the rest of your life the best of your life?

The Bible says, *"What a gift life is to those who stay the course!"* (James 5:11, MSG). So don't get distracted. Don't give in to panic or worry or hopelessness. Just fix your eyes on God's promise that he sees you, he cares for you, and he is working out his purpose in you. When everything is changing and uncertain, focusing regularly on God's unchanging truth and character found in his Word will help you see the way forward. God's love and good plan will become the driving force of your life, and you will find hope and peace for the future.

Once you start and maintain a daily habit in the Word, you're going to be amazed by how much this simple practice will strengthen your life. The better you get to know God, the more you will love him! In fact, the main objective of your time with God isn't to study *about* him but to actually spend time *with* him. It's not study time; it's relationship time!

When you set aside time every day to give devotion to God, three things happen:

- **You get direction from God.** He's not going to show you your life from beginning to end, because if God did reveal everything, it might scare you. His Word is like a scroll that he unrolls a little at a time, and as you do what he says, he unrolls a little bit more. That's why it's good to pray Psalm 25:4-5: *"Show me the* *path where I should go, O Lord; point out the right road for me to walk. Lead me; teach me"* (TLB).

- **You gain delight in God.** When you're going through a tough time and you're struggling to feel happy, the antidote is really simple: Get in the presence of God. Psalm 16:11 says, *"You make known to me the path of life; you will fill me with joy in your presence, with eternal pleasures at your right hand"* (NIV).

- **You grow more like Christ.** You can always tell which people have been spending a lot of time with Jesus—*because they're more like Jesus!* They're gentle and humble, patient and self-controlled. They *"speak the truth in love, growing in every way more and more like Christ"* (Ephesians 4:15, NLT).

WHAT'S DRIVING YOUR LIFE?

Keep this in mind: Daily time with God is a lifetime habit, so of course you'll miss a day here and there. It often takes three weeks to become familiar with a new task. Then it takes another three weeks before it becomes a comfortable habit. So don't get on a guilt trip or become legalistic about it. You live by grace, so don't punish yourself for skipping a day. It doesn't work that way. Since your time with God is about a relationship, it can't be run by rules.

And remember to commit everything to God in prayer. Simply pray: "God, I realize I was created to have fellowship with you. Thank you for making this privilege possible through Jesus' death. I know that daily fellowship with you is the most important thing in my life. I want to commit myself to spending time every day with you in a quiet time of Bible reading and prayer. I'm trusting in your strength to help me be consistent. In Jesus' name, amen."

NEXT STEPS

This is just the beginning!

I'm so glad you dedicated the past ten days to seeking God. I hope you'll continue that habit by reading my book *Daily Hope Devotional: 365 Days of Purpose, Peace, and Promise*. It blesses me to know that this devotional book will guide you every day to God and his Word, where you'll find real purpose, lasting peace, and faithful promises. You can also listen to my daily Bible teaching and find other resources to encourage you in your faith at PastorRick.com.

Look for *Daily Hope Devotional: 365 Days of Purpose, Peace, and Promise* wherever books are sold.

*A Fresh Start
through Salvation*

....

If you already know Jesus and have a relationship with him, that's great news! If not, the first step toward living a life driven by God's purposes is to accept Jesus as your Lord and Savior.

Surrendering your life to God is the ultimate fresh start!

Salvation is a free gift. You can have all your sins forgiven and get a free ticket to heaven. But while salvation is free to you, it is also costly—because somebody had to pay for it. When Jesus went to the cross, he paid the price for your sins to be forgiven.

NEXT STEPS

The truth is, everyone is full of sin. And a perfect God couldn't let you into his perfect home without an enormous price being paid for that sin. That's why it's not enough to be a good person. You need a Savior!

The Bible says, *"God says he will accept and acquit us—declare us 'not guilty'—if we trust Jesus Christ to take away our sins. And we all can be saved in this same way, by coming to Christ, no matter who we are or what we have been like"* (Romans 3:22, TLB).

You can come to Christ no matter who you are or what you've done. Start by saying a simple prayer like this: "God, I confess that I have sinned and gone my own way. I believe that Jesus died on the cross and rose from the grave so I wouldn't have to pay for my sin and so I could live forever with you. Please forgive me for the ways that I've messed up and accept me into your family. I want to turn every part of my life over to you. Help me to follow and serve you faithfully. In Jesus' name, amen."

If you just prayed this prayer, please write and tell me at Rick@PastorRick.com. I'd like to send you some free materials to help you start your journey with Jesus.

God's Promises to You

Trying to make a fresh start can lead to uncertainty. In such times, the key to stability is to focus on the truth of God's Word and his character. So as you seek to align your purposes with God's, tell yourself these unchangeable truths:

God sees everything I'm going through. *"The eyes of the LORD are on those who fear him, on those whose hope is in his unfailing love"* (Psalm 33:18, NIV).

God always acts from his goodness to me. *"And we know that in all things God works for the good of those who love him, who have been called according to his purpose"* (Romans 8:28, NIV).

God cares about everything I'm going through. *"I will watch for the LORD; I will wait confidently for God, who will save me. My God will hear me"* (Micah 7:7, GNT).

God's plan is always better than my plan. *"'For I know the plans I have for you,' says the LORD. 'They are plans for good and not for disaster, to give you a future and a hope'"* (Jeremiah 29:11, NLT).

God has the power to change what I'm going through. *"Ask, and you will be given what you ask for. Seek, and you will find. Knock, and the door will be opened"* (Matthew 7:7, TLB).

God will never stop loving me. *"For the mountains may move and the hills disappear, but even then my faithful love for you will remain"* (Isaiah 54:10, NLT).

Once I have put my trust in Jesus Christ, I cannot lose my salvation. *"I know the one in whom I trust, and I am sure that he is able to safely guard all that I have given him until the day of his return"* (2 Timothy 1:12, TLB).

No matter what I go through, God is with me. *"When you go through deep waters and great trouble, I will be with you. When you go through rivers of difficulty, you will not drown! When you walk through the fire of oppression, you will not be burned up—the flames will not consume you"* (Isaiah 43:2, TLB).

These passages only begin to express how much God wants to pour his love, grace, and forgiveness into your life. He has made you with a purpose, and he wants to fill you with his peace and help you stand on his promises. When you need an extra reminder of his care for you, I invite you to turn to the following pages.

*God Created You
with a Unique Purpose*

....

The Lord will work out his plans for
> my life—
for your faithful love, O Lord,
> endures forever.
Don't abandon me, for you made me.

PSALM 138:8 (NLT)

Trust in the Lord with all your heart;
> do not depend on your own
> > understanding.
Seek his will in all you do,
> and he will show you which path
> > to take.

PROVERBS 3:5-6 (NLT)

WHAT'S DRIVING YOUR LIFE?

We humans keep brainstorming options
   and plans,
      but God's purpose prevails.

PROVERBS 19:21 (MSG)

Above all pursue his kingdom and
righteousness, and all these things will
be given to you as well.

MATTHEW 6:33 (NET)

We must quickly carry out the tasks
assigned us by the one who sent us.
The night is coming, and then no one
can work.

JOHN 9:4 (NLT)

The most important thing is that I
complete my mission, the work that
the Lord Jesus gave me.

ACTS 20:24 (NCV)

GOD CREATED YOU WITH A UNIQUE PURPOSE

Give yourselves completely to God—every part of you—for you are back from death and you want to be tools in the hands of God, to be used for his good purposes.

ROMANS 6:13 (TLB)

My dear brothers and sisters, be steadfast, immovable, always excelling in the Lord's work, because you know that your labor in the Lord is not in vain.

1 CORINTHIANS 15:58 (CSB)

We are God's handiwork, created in Christ Jesus to do good works, which God prepared in advance for us to do.

EPHESIANS 2:10 (NIV)

Be generous with the different things God gave you, passing them around so

WHAT'S DRIVING YOUR LIFE?

all get in on it: if words, let it be God's words; if help, let it be God's hearty help. That way, God's bright presence will be evident in everything through Jesus, and *he'll* get all the credit as the One mighty in everything—encores to the end of time. Oh, yes!

1 PETER 4:10-11 (MSG)

God Fills You with Lasting Peace

....

Be strong and courageous. Do not be afraid or terrified . . . for the Lord your God goes with you; he will never leave you nor forsake you.

DEUTERONOMY 31:6 (NIV)

In peace I will lie down and sleep,
 for you alone, O Lord, will keep
 me safe.

PSALM 4:8 (NLT)

Abundant peace belongs to those who love your instruction; nothing makes them stumble.

PSALM 119:165 (CSB)

WHAT'S DRIVING YOUR LIFE?

You, Lord, give perfect peace
    to those who keep their purpose firm
    and put their trust in you.

ISAIAH 26:3 (GNT)

"For the mountains may move
    and the hills disappear,
but even then my faithful love for you
    will remain.
    My covenant of blessing will never be
    broken,"
says the Lord, who has mercy on you.

ISAIAH 54:10 (NLT)

He shall stand and shepherd his flock in
    the strength of the Lord,
    in the majesty of the name of the
    Lord his God.
And they shall dwell secure, for now
    he shall be great

GOD FILLS YOU WITH LASTING PEACE

to the ends of the earth.
And he shall be their peace.

MICAH 5:4-5 (ESV)

I have told you these things so that in me you may have peace. You will have suffering in this world. Be courageous! I have conquered the world.

JOHN 16:33 (CSB)

Now that we have been made right with God by putting our trust in Him, we have peace with Him. It is because of what our Lord Jesus Christ did for us.

ROMANS 5:1 (NLV)

I pray that God, the source of hope, will fill you completely with joy and peace because you trust in him. Then you will overflow with confident hope through the power of the Holy Spirit.

ROMANS 15:13 (NLT)

Do not worry. Learn to pray about everything. Give thanks to God as you ask Him for what you need. The peace of God is much greater than the human mind can understand. This peace will keep your hearts and minds through Christ Jesus.

PHILIPPIANS 4:6-7 (NLV)

The peace that Christ gives is to guide you in the decisions you make; for it is to this peace that God has called you together in the one body. And be thankful.

COLOSSIANS 3:15 (GNT)

*God Protects You
with His Promises*

....

Deep in your hearts you know that the
Lord has kept every promise he ever
made to you. Not one of them has
been broken.

JOSHUA 23:14 (CEV)

I prayed to the Lord, and he answered me;
    he freed me from all my fears.
The oppressed look to him and are glad;
    they will never be disappointed.
The helpless call to him, and he answers;
    he saves them from all their troubles.

PSALM 34:4-6 (GNT)

WHAT'S DRIVING YOUR LIFE?

As high as the heavens are above
> the earth,
so great is his faithful love
toward those who fear him.
As far as the east is from the west,
so far has he removed
our transgressions from us.
As a father has compassion on his
> children,
so the Lord has compassion on those
> who fear him.
For he knows what we are made of,
remembering that we are dust.

PSALM 103:11-14 (CSB)

The faithful love of the Lord never ends!
> His mercies never cease.
Great is his faithfulness;
> his mercies begin afresh each morning.

LAMENTATIONS 3:22-23 (NLT)

GOD PROTECTS YOU WITH HIS PROMISES

Turn to God and be baptized, every one of you, in the name of Jesus Christ for the forgiveness of your sins, and you will receive the gift of the Holy Spirit. This promise is for you and your children. It is for everyone our Lord God will choose, no matter where they live.

ACTS 2:38-39 (CEV)

No matter how many promises God has made, they are "Yes" in Christ. And so through him the "Amen" is spoken by us to the glory of God.

2 CORINTHIANS 1:20 (NIV)

My God will supply your every need according to his glorious riches in Christ Jesus.

PHILIPPIANS 4:19 (NET)

WHAT'S DRIVING YOUR LIFE?

Let us hold tightly without wavering to the hope we affirm, for God can be trusted to keep his promise.

HEBREWS 10:23 (NLT)

Every good gift and every perfect gift is from above, coming down from the Father of lights, with whom there is no variation or shadow due to change.

JAMES 1:17 (ESV)

He has granted to us his precious and very great promises, so that through them you may become partakers of the divine nature, having escaped from the corruption that is in the world because of sinful desire.

2 PETER 1:4 (ESV)

Scripture Credits

....

Scripture quotations marked CEV are taken from the Contemporary English Version, copyright © 1991, 1992, 1995 by American Bible Society. Used by permission. Scripture quotations marked CSB are taken from the Christian Standard Bible,® copyright © 2017 by Holman Bible Publishers. Used by permission. Christian Standard Bible® and CSB® are federally registered trademarks of Holman Bible Publishers. Scripture quotations marked ESV are from The ESV® Bible (The Holy Bible, English Standard Version®), copyright © 2001 by Crossway, a publishing ministry of Good News Publishers. Used by permission. All rights reserved. Scripture quotations marked GNT are taken from the Good News Translation in Today's English Version, Second Edition, copyright © 1992 by American Bible Society. Used by permission. Scripture quotations marked MSG are taken from *The Message*, copyright © 1993, 2002, 2018 by Eugene H. Peterson. Used by permission of NavPress. All rights reserved. Represented by Tyndale House Publishers. Scripture quotations marked NCV are taken from the New Century Version.® Copyright © 2005 by Thomas Nelson, Inc. Used by permission. All rights reserved. Scripture quotations marked NET are taken from the New English Translation, NET Bible,® copyright ©1996–2017 by Biblical Studies Press, L.L.C. http://netbible.com. All rights reserved. Scripture quotations marked NIV are taken from the Holy Bible, *New International Version*,® *NIV.*® Copyright © 1973, 1978, 1984, 2011 by Biblica, Inc.® Used by permission. All rights reserved worldwide. Scripture quotations marked NLT are taken from the *Holy Bible*, New Living Translation, copyright © 1996, 2004, 2015 by Tyndale House Foundation. Used by permission of Tyndale House Publishers, Carol Stream, Illinois 60188. All rights reserved. Scripture quotations marked NLV are taken from the Holy Bible, New Life Version. Copyright © 1969–2003 by Christian Literature International, P. O. Box 777, Canby, OR 97013. Used by permission. Scripture quotations marked TLB are taken from *The Living Bible*, copyright © 1971 by Tyndale House Foundation. Used by permission of Tyndale House Publishers, Carol Stream, Illinois 60188. All rights reserved.

About the Author

Rick Warren and his wife, Kay, founded Saddleback Church, the Purpose Driven Network, the PEACE Plan, and Hope for Mental Health. Warren is the cofounder of Celebrate Recovery and executive director of Finishing the Task coalition. He is also the bestselling author of *The Purpose Driven Life* and *The Purpose Driven Church*. You can listen to *Pastor Rick's Daily Hope* broadcast or sign up for his free Daily Hope Devotional at PastorRick.com.

PASTOR RICK'S DAILY HOPE

Learn, Love, and Live the Word!

To encourage you as you move toward all God has for you, listen to **Pastor Rick's Daily Hope** on your favorite podcast platform or at **PastorRick.com**. It will inspire you to study God's Word and build a deep, meaningful relationship with him, which is essential to living the life you were meant to live.

Continue Your Journey . . .
Listen to Pastor Rick's Daily Hope on your favorite podcast platform or at PastorRick.com